Twenty to **Knit**

Tiny Christmas Toys to Knit

Sachiyo Ishii

Search Press

Dedication

I would like to dedicate this book to my dear cousin, Keiko Yamashita, with whom I share lots of childhood memories.

First published in 2018

Search Press Limited
Wellwood, North Farm Road,
Tunbridge Wells, Kent TN2 3DR

Text copyright © Sachiyo Ishii 2018

Photographs by Fiona Murray

Photographs and design copyright
© Search Press Ltd. 2018

ISBN: 978-1-78221-536-3

Publisher's Note

The Publishers and author can accept no responsibility for any consequences arising from the information, advice or instructions given in this publication.

Readers are permitted to reproduce any of the items in this book for their personal use, or for the purposes of selling for charity, free of charge and without the prior permission of the Publishers. Any use of the items for commercial purposes is not permitted without the prior permission of the Publishers.

Suppliers

If you have difficulty in obtaining any of the materials and equipment mentioned in this book, then please visit the Search Press website for details of suppliers: www.searchpress.com

Printed in China through Asia Pacific Offset

Contents

Introduction

Christmas Day is only one day out of a whole year, but we make an enormous effort to prepare for this day. We decorate the house, buy gifts and stock up on food and drink. This task can be quite stressful and many of us find ourselves exhausted by the time the day arrives; however, we repeat this process year after year. Christmas is special, and we enjoy it very much.

Come November every year, I start knitting for Christmas. I pull out red, green and white fleecy yarn from my stash and make good use of it. I make little animals and dolls all dressed up for the occasion. It is such a joy to create these characters and it certainly gets me into the spirit. They all seem to find their perfect place in the end: by the fireplace, hanging on the Christmas tree, in a stocking or nicely boxed and wrapped for someone as a gift. I get to have lots of fun designing and creating and I am greeted with smiles later – it's a win-win situation.

I have collected my ideas to share in this book. Some look more complicated than others, but they are all quick knits. Start something simple to get the hang of knitting small toys. The actual knitting skills needed are simple – you only need to know how to knit and purl.

There is also some room for improvization. You can change the finished size simply by changing the yarn weight and needle size. Experiment with different fibres and textures to make your very own personalized knits. Each of your creations is precious and priceless. I am sure they will bring lots of happiness to you and your loved ones and they are perfect for the festive season.

Happy knitting and Merry Christmas!

Knitting know-how

Yarn

All the toys in this book are knitted with double knitting (DK/8-ply/light worsted) yarn. You do not need much yarn to create each toy and they are perfect for using up yarn already in your stash. I prefer to knit with DK (8-ply/light worsted) yarn, but you can use any weight you like. Adjust the needle size accordingly.

I have used mainly 100 per cent wool yarns in the projects, as I love the feel of wool and the subtle colour tones it can create. If you are making toys for children, you might wish to choose natural materials. I also find wool is the easiest when you want to make stitches neat and even. Feel free to experiment with alpaca, mohair, cotton or synthetic yarn for different textures. You may want to add some bright colours. I have also used chunky, fleecy yarn for some projects. This can be replaced with mohair or bouclé yarn if you prefer. If you need only small quantities of certain colours, tapestry wool is a good choice.

Stuffing

I have used polyester toy stuffing, which is readily available from most craft shops and online craft stores.

Knitting needles

All the toys in this book were made using double-pointed 2.75mm (UK 12, US 2) knitting needles, unless otherwise indicated. The resulting pieces are not too large and I found the needle size easy to work with. All items are knitted flat and sewn up at the end – you do not need to knit in the round.

You will need double-pointed needles (DPN) to make i-cords (the method is explained right); however, if you only have straight needles, simply work in stocking stitch (US stockinette stitch) and sew the sides together. Your knitting tension (gauge) needs to be fairly tight so that when the toys are sewn up, the toy stuffing is not visible through the stitches. If you find that you struggle to knit with DK (8-ply/light worsted) yarn on fine needles, experiment with slightly larger needles. Some knitters knit more tightly than others, and the tension (gauge) can also differ depending on the yarn you use. I have not specified tension (gauge) for any of the projects, as the size of the finished toys does not really matter.

Sewing your work together

I recommend that you use a chenille or other needle with a sharp point, as it is easier to work through your tightly knitted toys than a blunt-ended needle. You can also use the same needle for embroidering features on the toys. Your toys will be sewn up using the same yarn that you knitted them with, so it is a good idea to make a habit of leaving fairly long yarn ends when you cast on and cast off. Join the seams using mattress stitch with right sides facing outwards.

Other tools

Wooden chopstick

A simple but incredibly effective tool, a chopstick is by far the best instrument for pushing stuffing into your toys. If you do not have one, you could use a large knitting needle or a pencil.

Scissors

A pair of sharp scissors is essential for trimming yarn ends when sewing up your projects.

Stitches used

Unless specified otherwise, all patterns are worked in stocking stitch (US stockinette stitch). Other stitches used for making features for the toys are described below and are extremely simple. They include garter stitch, i-cords, French knots, backstitch and chain stitch.

Garter stitch

Knit every row. You can also purl every row.

I-cords

I-cords are used for some of the body parts. Using DPN, cast on the required number of stitches. Do not turn. Slide the stitches to the opposite end of the needle, then knit the stitches again, taking the yarn firmly across the back of the work. Repeat to the desired length. Break yarn and thread through the stitches or cast off, as instructed in the pattern.

French knots

These are used for most of the figures' and animals' eyes. Thread your needle with yarn and bring it up from the back where you want to make a knot. Holding the needle firmly, wrap the yarn around it twice. Push the needle through to the back of the project, leaving the French knot on the surface.

Backstitch

This stitch is used to embroider facial features and to create hair. Thread the yarn through the needle. Bring the needle from the back to the front of the work. Insert the needle from front to back and repeat.

Chain stitch

This stitch forms a row of continuous chains. Bring your needle to the front of the work. Insert the needle next to where you first came up and poke the end of it up through the fabric. Loop the yarn under the needle and pull through to create the first link of the chain. Repeat.

Abbreviations

The abbreviations listed below are the most frequently used terms in the book. Any special abbreviations in a pattern are explained on the relevant page.

DPN	double-pointed needles
g st	garter stitch
k	knit
kfb	knit into the front and back of the stitch, making one more stitch
k2tog	knit 2 stitches together
p	purl
p2tog	purl 2 stitches together
rep	repeat
RS	right side(s)
skpo	slip 1, knit 1, pass slipped stitch over
sl 1	slip one stitch from the left-hand needle to the right-hand needle without working it
st(s)	stitch(es)
st st	stocking/stockinette stitch
WS	wrong sides(s)
yb	yarn back
yf	yarn forward

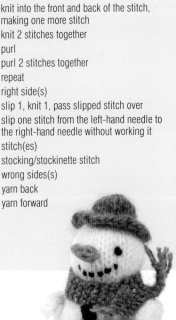

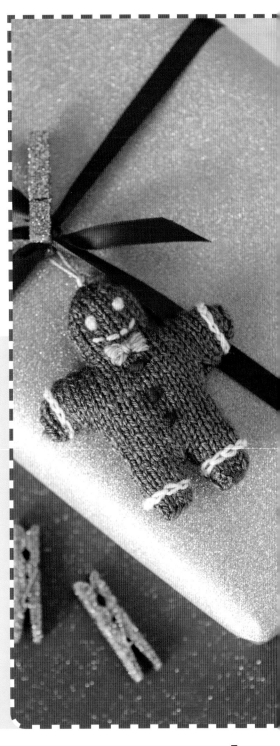

Polar Bears

Materials:

30m (33yd) of DK (8-ply/light worsted) yarn in white (A) and small amounts in red felted tweed (B) and lilac felted tweed (D)

Small amount of 4-ply (fingering) yarn in dark brown (C)

Small amount of toy stuffing

Size:

Mummy bear: 9cm (3½in)

Baby bear: 6cm (2¼in)

Instructions:

Mummy's body and head

Using yarn A, cast on 10 sts.

Row 1 (WS): p to end.

Row 2: (kfb) to end (20 sts).

Row 3: p to end.

Row 4: (k1, kfb) to end (30 sts).

Row 5: p to end.

Row 6: cast on 6 sts, k to end (36 sts).

Row 7: cast on 6 sts, p to end (42 sts).

Rows 8–17: beg with a k RS row, work 10 rows in st st.

Row 18: k2tog, k to last 2 sts, k2tog (40 sts).

Row 19: p to end.

Rows 20–29: rep rows 18 and 19 five more times (30 sts).

Row 30: (k3, k2tog) to end (24 sts).

Rows 31–37: beg with a p WS row, work 7 rows in st st.

Row 38: (k4, k2tog) to end (20 sts).

Rows 39–41: beg with a p WS row, work 3 rows in st st.

Row 42: (k3, k2tog) to end (16 sts).

Rows 43–45: beg with a p WS row, work 3 rows in st st.

Row 46: k4, (k2tog, k1) three times, k3 (13 sts).

Rows 47–49: beg with a p WS row, work 3 rows in st st.

Break yarn, thread through all sts and pull tightly. Fasten off.

Tail

Using yarn A, cast on 9 sts. Beg with a p WS row, work 4 rows in st st.

Break yarn, thread through all sts and pull tightly. Fasten off.

Scarf

Using yarn B, cast on 4 sts, leaving a long end. Work in g st until piece measures 20cm (8in). Cast off, leaving a long end. Thread a needle with the yarn end and backstitch along the short edge a few times, leaving a loop every other stitch. Cut the loops open to make the fringe. Repeat for the other edge.

To make up

Fold the bottom corners inwards and sew the edges together to create the hind legs. Sew the body seam and stuff. Seam and stuff the tail, then sew the tail in place on the body. Thread a needle with a length of yarn A and backstitch in the same spot on the head three times for each ear. Using yarn C, work a French knot for each eye and embroider the nose and mouth with backstitches. Sew the scarf around the bear's neck.

Baby's body and head

Using yarn A, cast on 8 sts.

Row 1 (WS): p to end.

Row 2: (kfb) to end (16 sts).

Row 3: p to end.

Row 4: (k1, kfb) to end (24 sts).

Row 5: p to end.

Row 6: cast on 4 sts, k to end (28 sts).

Row 7: cast on 4 sts, p to end (32 sts).

Rows 8–13: beg with a k RS row, work 6 rows in st st.

Row 14: k2tog, k to last 2 sts, k2tog (30 sts).

Row 15: p to end.

Rows 16–21: rep rows 14 and 15 three more times (24 sts).

Row 22: (k4, k2tog) to end (20 sts).

Rows 23–27: beg with a p WS row, work 5 rows in st st.

Row 28: (k3, k2tog) to end (16 sts).

Rows 29–31: beg with a p WS row, work 3 rows in st st.

Row 32: k3, (k2tog, k1, k2tog) twice, k3 (12 sts).

Rows 33–35: beg with a p WS row, work 3 rows in st st.

Break yarn, thread through all sts and pull tightly. Fasten off.

Scarf

Using yarn D, cast on 3 sts, leaving a long end. Work in g st until piece measures 13cm (5¼in). Cast off, leaving a long end. Thread a needle with the yarn end and backstitch along the short edge a few times, leaving a loop every other stitch. Cut the loops open to make the fringe. Repeat for the other edge.

To make up

Make up as given for the Mummy polar bear, omitting the tail.

Gingerbread House

Materials:

16m (17½yd) of DK (8-ply/light worsted) yarn in honey yellow (A) and brown (B), 10m (11yd) in white (C) and a small amount in dark brown (D)

Small amounts of 4-ply (fingering) yarn in green (E), red (F) and white (G)

Small amount of toy stuffing

5 x 3.5cm (2 x 1¼in) piece of cardboard (optional)

Additional equipment:

2.75mm (UK 12, US 2) DPN to make i-cord

3.5mm (UK 9/10, US 4) knitting needles

Size:

8cm (3in)

Instructions:

Note: All parts are knitted with 2.75mm (UK 12, US 2) needles except the roof.

House

Using yarn A, cast on 54 sts.

Row 1 (WS): k to end.

Row 2: k1, p10, k1, p15, k1, p10, k1, p15.

Rows 3–8: rep rows 1 and 2 three more times.

Row 9: p to end.

Row 10: cast off 12 sts (1 st on left needle), p14, turn. Work in short rows over these 15 sts only as follows:

Row 11: k1, skpo, k to last 3 sts, k2tog, k1 (13 sts).

Row 12: beg with a p WS row, work 3 rows in st st over short row sts ONLY.

Rep last 4 rows four more times (5 sts).

Next row: k1, k3tog, k1 (3 sts).

Next row: p1, p2tog (2 sts).

Pass the first st over the second and fasten off.

With WS facing, rejoin yarn to remaining sts and rep from row 10 above once more.

Base panel

Using yarn B, cast on 17 sts.

Work 20 rows in g st. Cast off.

Roof

Using two strands of yarn B held together and 3.5mm (UK 9/10, US 4) needles, cast on 9 sts.

Work in g st until the piece measures 12cm (4¾in). Cast off.

Candy stick on roof: make two

Using yarn C, cast on 8 sts. Work in st st until the piece measures 11cm (4¼in). Cast off.

Candy around door

Using yarn C, cast on 4 sts. Work an i-cord until the piece measures 7.5cm (3in). Break yarn, thread through all sts and pull tightly. Fasten off.

Door

Using yarn D, cast on 6 sts.

Beg with a p WS row, work 7 rows in st st.

Row 8: skpo, k2, k2tog (4 sts).

Row 9: (p2tog) twice (2 sts).

Row 10: k2tog (1 st). Fasten off.

Leaves: make two

Using yarn E, cast on 6 sts.

Rows 1–3: k to end.

Row 4: k1, (k2tog) twice, k1 (4 sts).

Row 5: k to end.

Row 6: (k2tog) twice (2 sts).

Row 7: k2tog (1 st). Fasten off.

Berries: make two

Using yarn F, cast on 10 sts. Break yarn, thread through all sts and pull tightly. Fasten off.

Stitch the sides together to create a berry.

Round candy above door

Using yarn G, cast on 15 sts.

Row 1 (WS): (using yarn G p1, using yarn E p1) to end.

Rows 2–6: changing colours as set and beg with a k RS row, work 5 rows in st st. Break yarn E.

Rows 7 and 8: using yarn G and beg with a p WS row, work 2 rows in st st.

Break yarn, thread through all sts and pull tightly.

Sew the side seam and stuff. Thread a needle with yarn G, pierce centre from base to top, top to base and repeat. Pull yarn gently to flatten both ends.

To make up

Sew the side seam of the house. Sew the base panel to the bottom edge of the house, insert the cardboard so it lies flat on the base and stuff. Sew the roof in place. Using yarn C, embroider criss-cross lines on the roof using long backstitches. Thread a needle with yarn F and wrap it around the roof candy stick, securing with a few stitches. Repeat with yarn E. Work the same way for the candy around the front door, using yarn F only. Attach the candy sticks to the roof. Attach the leaves and berries. Attach the round candy, door and candy sticks to the front panel.

Mini Stocking

Materials:

10m (11yd) of DK (8-ply/light worsted) yarn in red (B)
and small amounts in white (A), light brown (C),
cream (D), dark brown (E), light blue (F) and blue (G)

Small amount of toy stuffing

Additional equipment:

2.75mm (UK 12, US 2) DPN to make i-cord

Size:

7cm (2¾in) long

Instructions:

Stocking

Using yarn A, cast on 30 sts.

Row 1 (RS): (k1, p1) to end.

Row 2: (k1, p1) to end.

Rows 3 and 4: rep rows 1 and 2
once more. Break yarn A.

Rows 5–16: change to yarn B and,
beg with a k RS row, work 12 rows
in st st.

Shape the heel with short rows
as follows:

Row 17: k20, yf, sl1, yb, turn.

Row 18: sl1, p10, yb, sl1, yf, turn.

Row 19: sl1, k11, yf, sl1, yb, turn.

Row 20: sl1, p12, yb, sl1, yf, turn.

Row 21: sl1, k13, yf, sl1, yb, turn.

Row 22: sl1, p14, yb, sl1, yf, turn.

Row 23: sl1, k15, yf, sl1, yb, turn.

Row 24: sl1, p16, yb, sl1, yf, turn.

Row 25: sl1, k17, yf, sl1, yb, turn.

Row 26: p to end.

Rows 27–30: beg with a k RS row,
work 4 rows in st st.

Row 31: (k3, k2tog) to end (24 sts).

Row 32: p to end.

Row 33: (k2, k2tog) to end (18 sts).

Row 34: p to end.

Row 35: k2, (k2tog, k2) to end
(14 sts).

Cast off purlwise.

To make up

Seam the sides and attach a loop of
yarn A to the top for hanging.

Teddy

Using yarn C, cast on 8 sts.

Row 1 (WS): p to end.

Row 2: (kfb) to end (16 sts).

Rows 3–7: beg with a p WS row,
work 5 rows in st st.

Row 8 (shape neck): k1, (k2tog, k1)
to end (11 sts).

Row 9: p to end.

Row 10: k3, (kfb) five times, k3
(16 sts).

Rows 11–16: beg with a p WS row,
work 6 rows in st st.

Row 17: (p2tog) to end (8 sts).

Break yarn, thread through all sts and
pull tightly. Fasten off.

Ears: make two

Using yarn C, cast on 5 sts. Break
yarn, thread through all sts and pull
tightly. Fasten off.

Muzzle

Using yarn D, cast on 10 sts. Break
yarn, thread through all sts and pull
tightly. Fasten off.

To make up

Seam the body and stuff, avoiding
the neck area. Using yarn C, work a
running stitch around the neck and
pull tightly to gather. With fastened-off
yarn end, seam the muzzle up to the
cast-on edge. Attach the cast-on edge
of the muzzle to the front of the face.
Sew the ears to the head. Using yarn
E, work a French knot for each eye
and embroider the nose with a few
short backstitches.

Gift box

Using yarn F, cast on 8 sts. Beg with a
p WS row, work in st st until the piece
measures 7cm (2¾in). Cast off.

To make up

With WS facing, fold a third from the
bottom and cover it with a third from
the top. Secure the piece with a few
stitches. Using yarn G, make a ribbon
and tie a bow at the front centre.

Candy

Using yarn B, cast on 4 sts. Work an
i-cord, alternating 2 rows in yarn B
and 2 rows in yarn A, until the piece
measures 7cm (2¾in).

Break yarn, thread through all sts and
pull tightly. Fasten off.

To make up

With the fastened-off yarn end, work
a running stitch through the body
and pull gently to shape. Hide the
yarn ends inside the candy. Finally,
place the gifts inside the stocking and
secure the items in place with a few
stitches if desired.

Rudolf

Materials:

10m (11yd) of DK (8-ply/light worsted) yarn in brown (A) and small amounts in red brown (B), red (C), black (D) and green (E)

5mm (¼in) diameter gold bell

Small amount of toy stuffing

Size:

7cm (2¾in) long

Instructions:

Body

Using yarn A and, starting with the hind legs, cast on 18 sts.

Rows 1–6: beg with a k RS row, work 6 rows in st st.

Row 7: cast off 2 sts, k to end (16 sts).

Row 8: cast off 2 sts, p to end (14 sts).

Row 9: cast on 2 sts, k to end (16 sts).

Row 10: cast on 2 sts, p to end (18 sts).

Rows 11 and 12: beg with a k RS row, work 2 rows in st st.

Row 13: cast off 2 sts, k5, (kfb) twice, k to end (18 sts).

Row 14: cast off 2 sts, p to end (16 sts).

Row 15: cast on 3 sts, k7, (kfb) twice, k to end (21 sts).

Row 16: cast on 3 sts, p to end (24 sts).

Row 17: k11, (kfb) twice, k to end (26 sts).

Rows 18–20: beg with a p WS row, work 3 rows in st st.

Row 21: cast off 8 sts, k to end (18 sts).

Row 22: cast off 8 sts, p to end (10 sts).

Row 23: cast on 4 sts, k to end (14 sts).

Row 24: cast on 4 sts, p to end (18 sts).

Rows 25 and 26: beg with a k RS row, work 2 rows in st st.

Row 27: skpo, k to last 2 sts, k2tog (16 sts).

Cast off.

Ears: make two

Using yarn A, cast on 4 sts.

Row 1: (p2tog) twice (2 sts).

Row 2: skpo (1 st).

Fasten off.

Tail

Using yarn A, cast on 3 sts. Beg with a p WS row, work 2 rows in st st.

Break yarn, thread through all sts and pull tightly. Fasten off.

Antlers: make two

Using yarn B, cast on 15 sts. Cast off 4 sts, transfer stitch on right needle back to left needle, cast on 3 sts, cast off 8 sts (the 3 cast-on sts and 5 original sts), transfer stitch on right needle back to left needle, cast on 3 sts, cast off all sts.

Nose

Using yarn C, cast on 4 sts. Break yarn, thread through all sts and pull tightly. Fasten off.

Stitch the sides together to create a nose.

To make up

Sew each hind leg from the tip and sew the under-body flaps closed to the cast-on edge. Sew each front leg from the tip and front edge of the under-body flaps. Sew the underside of the neck and head seams. Stuff the body and close the tummy. Attach the nose and antlers to the head. Seam the tail and attach it to the end of the body. Using yarn D, work a French knot for each eye. Thread a gold bell onto a length of yarn E, wrap it around the neck and tie the ends to secure.

Santa and Sack

Materials:

14m (15½yd) of DK (8-ply/light worsted) yarn in red (A) and small amounts in beige (C), black (D), brown (E), dark brown (F) and white (G)

Small amount of chunky (bulky) fleecy yarn in white (B)

Small amount of toy stuffing

Size:

9cm (3½in) tall

Instructions:

Body and head

Using yarn A, cast on 9 sts.

Row 1 (WS): p to end.

Row 2: (kfb) in each st to end (18 sts).

Row 3: p to end.

Row 4: (k1, kfb) to end (27 sts).

Row 5: p to end.

Row 6 (g st ridge): p to end.

Rows 7–9: beg with a p WS row, work 3 rows in st st. Do not break yarn.

Rows 10 and 11 (g st ridge): change to yarn B and k to end. Break yarn B.

Rows 12–23: using yarn A, beg with a k RS row, work 12 rows in st st.

Row 24 (shape neck): (k2tog) to last st, k1 (14 sts). Break yarn A.

Row 25: change to yarn C and p to end.

Row 26: k4, (kfb) six times, k4 (20 sts).

Rows 27–30: beg with a p WS row, work 4 rows in st st.

Row 31 (shape eyeline): p4, (p2tog, p1) four times, p4 (16 sts).

Rows 32–34: beg with a k RS row, work 3 rows in st st.

Row 35: (k2, k2tog) to end (12 sts).

Break yarn, thread through all sts and pull tightly. Fasten off.

Hat

Using yarn B, cast on 18 sts. Break yarn B.

Rows 1–8: using yarn A, beg with a k RS row, work 8 rows in st st.

Row 9: (k2, k2tog) four times, k2 (14 sts).

Rows 10–12: beg with a p WS row, work 3 rows in st st.

Row 13: k2tog, (k1, k2tog) to end (9 sts).

Break yarn, thread through all sts and pull tightly. Fasten off.

Beard

Using yarn B, cast on 10 sts.

Row 1: k to end.

Row 2: skpo, k to last 2 sts, k2tog (8 sts).

Rows 3–5: rep row 2 three more times (2 sts).

Row 6: k2tog (1 st).

Fasten off.

Arms: make two

Using yarn A, cast on 8 sts.

Rows 1 and 2: beg with a p WS row, work 2 rows in st st. Do not break yarn.

Rows 3 and 4 (g st ridge): change to yarn B and p to end. Break yarn B.

Rows 5–10: using yarn A, beg with a p WS row, work 6 rows in st st.

Break yarn, thread through all sts and pull tightly. Fasten off.

Shoes: make two

Using yarn D, cast on 8 sts.

Row 1 (WS): p to end.

Row 2: (kfb) to end (16 sts).

Rows 3–7: beg with a p WS row, work 5 rows in st st.

Row 8: (k2tog) to end (8 sts).

Break yarn, thread through all sts and pull tightly. Fasten off.

Sack

Using yarn E, cast on 30 sts.

Rows 1–17: beg with a p WS row, work 17 rows in st st.

Row 18: (k2tog) to end (15 sts).

Row 19: p to end.

Row 20: (kfb) to end (30 sts).

Rows 21–23: beg with a p WS row, work 3 rows in st st.

Cast off.

To make up

With the fastened-off yarn end, sew the body seam closed from the head down to the neck. Keep this yarn end free at the neck. With the cast-on yarn end, work a running stitch along the cast-on edge of the body and pull tightly to gather. Sew the body closed from the base up to the waist. Stuff and sew the rest of the body seam closed, avoiding the neck area. With the yarn C end left at the neck, work a running stitch around the neck and pull tightly to gather. Using the same yarn, work a running stitch on the face over the eyeline and pull gently to shape a dent. Make a French knot in yarn C for the nose.

Thread a needle with yarn A and insert it from the centre of the base, taking the needle out at the back of the body. Repeat with the other yarn end and pull on the yarn ends to flatten the base. Seam the shoes and stuff. Attach the shoes to the base of the body. Seam and stuff the arms and attach them to the sides of the body. Sew the beard in place on the face. Seam the hat and attach it to the head. Using yarn F, work a French knot for each eye. Using yarn G, work two French knots for buttons on the front of the body. Seam the sack, stuff lightly and work a running stitch along the decrease row. Attach the bag to one hand.

Mary and Baby Jesus

Materials:

For Mary: 10m (11yd) of DK (8-ply/light worsted) yarn in light blue (A) and small amounts in pale pink (B) and dark brown (D)

Small amount of 4-ply (fingering) yarn in light brown (C)

For Baby Jesus: 8m (9yd) of DK (8-ply/light worsted) yarn in white (A) and a small amount in beige (B)

Small amount of 4-ply (fingering) yarn in dark brown (C)

Small amount of toy stuffing for both figures

Size:

Mary: 7cm (2¾in) tall

Baby Jesus: 6cm (2¼in) long

Instructions:

Mary's body and head

Using yarn A, cast on 10 sts.

Row 1 (WS): p to end.

Row 2: (kfb) to end (20 sts).

Row 3: p to end.

Row 4: (k1, kfb) to end (30 sts).

Row 5: p to end.

Row 6: (k2, kfb) to end (40 sts).

Rows 7–15: beg with a p WS row, work 9 rows in st st.

Row 16: (k2, k2tog) to end (30 sts).

Rows 17–21: beg with a p WS row, work 5 rows in st st.

Row 22: (k1, k2tog) to end (20 sts).

Rows 23–25: beg with a p WS row, work 3 rows in st st.

Row 26 (shape neck): (k2tog) to end (10 sts). Break yarn A.

Row 27: change to yarn B and p to end.

Row 28: k1, (kfb) eight times, k1 (18 sts).

Rows 29–31: beg with a p WS row, work 3 rows in st st.

Row 32 (shape eyeline): k3, (k2tog, k1) four times, k3 (14 sts).

Rows 33–35: beg with a p WS row, work 3 rows in st st.

Row 36: k2, (k2tog, k2) to end (11 sts).

Break yarn, thread through all sts and pull tightly. Fasten off.

Hood

Using yarn A, cast on 22 sts.

Beg with a p WS row, work 9 rows in st st.

Cast off.

To make up

With fastened-off yarn end, sew the body seam closed from the head down to the neck. Keep this yarn end free at the neck. With cast-on yarn end, work a running stitch along cast-on edge of the body and pull tightly to gather. Sew the body closed from the base up to the waist. Stuff and sew the rest of the body seam closed, avoiding the neck area. With the yarn B tail end left at the neck, work a running stitch around the neck and pull tightly to gather. With the same yarn, work a running stitch on the face over the eyeline and pull gently to shape a dent. Make a French knot in yarn B for the nose. Thread a needle with yarn A and insert it from the centre of the base, taking the needle out at the front of the body. Repeat with the other yarn end and pull on the yarn ends to flatten the base and shape the lap. For the hair, thread a needle with yarn C and make backstitches on the forehead. Using yarn D, work a French knot for each eye. Seam and attach the hood.

Baby Jesus' body and head

Using yarn A, cast on 10 sts.

Row 1 (WS): p to end.

Row 2: (kfb) to end (20 sts).

Rows 3–15: beg with a p WS row, work 13 rows in st st.

Row 16 (shape neck): (k2tog) to end (10 sts). Break yarn A.

Row 17: change to yarn B and p to end.

Row 18: k2, (kfb) six times, k2 (16 sts).

Rows 19–21: beg with a p WS row, work 3 rows in st st.

Row 22 (shape eyeline): k3, (k2tog, k1) three times, k2tog, k2 (12 sts).

Rows 23–25: beg with a p WS row, work 3 rows in st st.

Rows 26: (k2, k2tog) to end (9 sts).

Break yarn, thread through all sts and pull tightly. Fasten off.

Hood

Using yarn A, cast on 18 sts.

Beg with a p WS row, work 9 rows in st st.

Cast off.

To make up

Make up the head and body as given for Mary. Using yarn C, embroider the eyes with backstitches. Seam and attach the hood. Finally, attach Baby Jesus to Mary's lap with a few stitches.

Joseph

Materials:

10m (11yd) of DK (8-ply/light worsted) yarn in purple felted tweed (A) and small amounts in beige (B) and dark brown (D)

Small amount of DK (8-ply/light worsted) bouclé yarn in grey (C)

Small amount of toy stuffing

Size:

9cm (3½in) tall

Instructions:

Body and head

Using yarn A, cast on 10 sts.

Work rows 1–21 as given for Mary (see page 18).

Rows 22–25: beg with a k RS row, work 4 rows in st st.

Row 26: (k1, k2tog) to end (20 sts).

Rows 27–29: beg with a p WS row, work 3 rows in st st.

Row 30 (shape neck): (k2tog) to end (10 sts). Break yarn A.

Row 31: change to yarn B, k1, (kfb) eight times, k1 (18 sts).

Rows 32–34: beg with a p WS row, work 3 rows in st st.

Row 35 (shape eyeline): k3, (k2tog, k1) four times, k3 (14 sts).

Rows 36–38: beg with a p WS row, work 3 rows in st st.

Row 39: k2, (k2tog, k2) to end (11 sts).

Break yarn, thread through all sts and pull tightly. Fasten off.

Hood

Using yarn A, cast on 22 sts.

Beg with a p WS row, work 9 rows in st st.

Cast off.

To make up

With the fastened-off yarn end, sew the body seam closed from the head down to the neck. Keep this yarn end free at the neck. With the cast-on yarn end, work a running stitch along the cast-on edge of the body and pull tightly to gather. Sew the body closed from the base up to the waist. Stuff and sew the rest of the body seam closed, avoiding the neck area. With the yarn B tail end left at the neck, work a running stitch around the neck and pull tightly to gather. With the same yarn, work a running stitch on the face over the eyeline and pull gently to shape a dent. Make a French knot using yarn B for the nose. Thread a needle with yarn A and insert it from the centre of the base, taking the needle out at the front of the body. Repeat with the other yarn end and pull on the yarn ends to flatten the base. To make the hair and beard, thread a needle with yarn C and make backstitches, leaving short loops. Using yarn D, work a French knot for each eye. Seam and attach the hood.

Christmas Elf

Materials:

8m (9yd) of DK (8-ply/light worsted) yarn in green (A) and small amounts in yellow (B), pale pink (C), sea green (D) and dark brown (F)

Small amount of 4-ply (fingering) yarn in brown (E)

Small amount of toy stuffing

Size:

9cm (3½in) tall

Instructions:

Body

Using yarn A, cast on 11 sts.

Row 1 (WS): p to end.

Row 2: (kfb) in each st to end (22 sts).

Row 3: p to end. Do not break yarn.

Row 4: change to yarn B and k to end.

Row 5 (g st ridge): using yarn B, k to end. Break yarn B.

Rows 6–15: using yarn A, beg with a k RS row, work 10 rows in st st. Break yarn A.

Row 16 (shape neck): change to yarn B, k1, (k2tog, k1) to end (15 sts).

Row 17 (g st ridge): using yarn B, k to end. Break yarn B.

Row 18: change to yarn C and k to end.

Row 19: p5, (pfb) five times, p5 (20 sts).

Rows 20–22: beg with a k RS row, work 3 rows in st st.

Row 23 (shape eyeline): p4, (p2tog, p1) four times, p4 (16 sts).

Rows 24–26: beg with a k RS row, work 3 rows in st st.

Row 27: (p2, p2tog) to end (12 sts).

Break yarn, thread through all sts and pull tightly. Fasten off.

Hat

Using yarn B, cast on 20 sts.

Row 1 (RS): k to end. Break yarn B.

Rows 2–4: change to yarn A and, beg with a p WS row, work 3 rows in st st.

Row 5: (k2tog, k2) to end (15 sts).

Rows 6–8: beg with a p WS row, work 3 rows in st st.

Row 9: (k2tog) to last st, k1 (8 sts).

Rows 10 and 11: beg with a p WS row, work 2 rows in st st.

Row 12: (p2tog) to end (4 sts).

Break yarn, thread through all sts and pull tightly. Fasten off.

Arms: make two

Using yarn A, cast on 7 sts.

Rows 1 and 2: beg with a p WS row, work 2 rows in st st. Do not break yarn.

Rows 3 and 4 (g st ridge): change to yarn B, p to end. Break yarn B.

Rows 5–9: using yarn A, beg with a p WS row, work 5 rows in st st.

Break yarn, thread through all sts and pull tightly. Fasten off.

Legs: make two

Using yarn D, cast on 12 sts.

Rows 1 and 2: beg with a p WS row, work 2 rows in st st.

Row 3: p3, (p2tog) three times, p3 (9 sts).

Row 4: k3, k3tog, k3 (7 sts). Break yarn D.

Rows 5–9: change to yarn A and, beg with a p WS row, work 5 rows in st st.

Break yarn, thread through all sts and pull tightly. Fasten off.

Ears: make two

Using yarn C, cast on 3 sts.

Row 1: p to end.

Row 2: k1, k2tog (2 sts).

Row 3: p2tog (1 st).

Fasten off.

To make up

With the fastened-off yarn end, sew the body seam closed from the head down to the neck. Keep this yarn end free at the neck. With the cast-on yarn end, work a running stitch along the cast-on edge of the body and pull tightly to gather. Sew the body closed from the base up to the waist. Stuff and sew the rest of the body seam closed. With the yarn C tail end left at the neck, work a running stitch around the neck and pull tightly to gather. With the same yarn, work a running stitch on the face over the eyeline and pull gently to shape a dent. Make a French knot using yarn C for the nose. Seam the legs and attach them to the base of the body. Sew the arms and ears in place. Seam the hat and secure it to the head. For the hair, make backstitches with yarn E, leaving small loops. Using yarn F, work a French knot for each eye. Using yarn B, French knot three buttons on the body.

Gingerbread Man

Materials:

10m (11yd) of DK (8-ply/light worsted) yarn in brown (A) and small amounts in red (C) and mint green (D)

Small amount of 4-ply (fingering) yarn in white (B)

Small amount of toy stuffing

Short length of string for hanging loop

Additional equipment:

A stitch holder or a spare needle

Size:

8cm (3in) tall

Instructions:

Front panel, first leg

Using yarn A, cast on 7 sts.

Rows 1–5: beg with a p WS row, work 5 rows in st st. Break yarn, place sts on a holder.

Second leg

Work as for first leg but do not break yarn.

Row 6 (joining row): k7, then k across held 7 sts of first leg (14 sts).

Rows 7–15: beg with a p WS row, work 9 rows in st st.

Row 16: cast on 5 sts, k to end (19 sts).

Row 17: cast on 5 sts, p to end (24 sts).

Rows 18–23: beg with a k RS row, work 6 rows in st st.

Row 24: cast off 7 sts, k to end (17 sts).

Row 25: cast off 7 sts, p to end (10 sts).

Row 26: cast on 5 sts, k to end (15 sts).

Row 27: cast on 5 sts, p to end (20 sts).

Rows 28–33: beg with a k RS row, work 6 rows in st st.

Row 34: (k2, k2tog) to end (15 sts).

Row 35: (p1, p2tog) to end (10 sts).

Break yarn, thread through all sts and pull tightly. Fasten off.

Back panel

Work as given for front panel to row 15.

Row 16: k to end.

Row 17: cast on 5 sts, p to end (19 sts).

Row 18: cast on 5 sts, k to end (24 sts).

Rows 19–24: beg with a p WS row, work 6 rows in st st. Cast off.

To make up

With the fastened-off yarn end of the front panel, sew the back seam of the head down to the neck. Sew all the side seams and lightly stuff. Using yarn B, embroider chain stitches on the front panel across the hands and feet, and make backstitches for the mouth. Using two strands of yarn B held together, work a French knot for each eye. Using yarn C, work three French knots down the body. Using yarn D, embroider a bow tie at the neck with long horizontal backstitches, gathered in the middle with a short vertical stitch. Using a length of string, attach a hanging loop if desired.

Owl

Materials:

10m (11yd) of DK (8-ply/light worsted) yarn in grey (A) and small amounts in red brown (B)

Small amounts of 4-ply (fingering) yarn in white (C), yellow (D) and dark brown (E)

Small amount of toy stuffing

Size:

6cm (2½in) tall

Instructions:

Body

Using yarn A, cast on 10 sts.

Row 1 (WS): p to end.

Row 2: (kfb) to end (20 sts).

Row 3: p to end.

Row 4: (k1, kfb) to end (30 sts).

Rows 5–15: beg with a p WS row, work 11 rows in st st.

Row 16: (k1, k2tog) to end (20 sts).

Rows 17–21: beg with a p WS row, work 5 rows in st st.

Row 22: (k2tog) to end (10 sts).

Break yarn, thread through all sts and pull tightly.

Fasten off.

Wings: make two

Using yarn E, cast on 10 sts.

Rows 1–4: beg with a p WS row, work 4 rows in st st.

Row 5: (p2tog) to end (5 sts).

Break yarn, thread through all sts and pull tightly.

Fasten off.

Eyes: make two

Using yarn C, cast on 16 sts.

Row 1 (WS): p to end.

Row 2: (k2tog) to end (8 sts).

Break yarn, thread through all sts and pull tightly.

Fasten off.

Ears: make two

Using yarn E, cast on 5 sts.

Row 1 (WS): p2tog, p1, p2tog (3 sts).

Row 2: sl1, k2tog, pass the first st over the second (1 st).

Fasten off.

Beak

Using yarn D, cast on 8 sts.

Row 1: p to end.

Row 2: (k2tog) to end (4 sts).

Break yarn, thread through all sts and pull tightly.

Fasten off.

Scarf

Using yarn B, cast on 3 sts. Work in g st until piece measures 14cm (5½in). Cast off.

To make up

Seam the body and stuff. Seam the wings and attach them to the sides of the body. Seam the sides of each eye to form circles then sew the eyes in place on the face. Seam the beak from the fastened-off end and sew the cast-on edge to the face. Thread a needle with the fastened-off yarn end of one ear, make a knot at the end and cut the yarn, leaving 5mm (¼in) for fluff. Repeat for the second ear, then sew the cast-on edge of the ears in place on the head. Using yarn E, embroider the eyes with backstitches. Attach the scarf around the neck. Using yarn D, embroider the feet with backstitches.

Christmas Bauble

Materials:

For one bauble: 6m (6½yd) of DK (8-ply/light worsted) yarn in pink (A), red (B) and white (C)

Small amount of yellow yarn or cord

Small amount of toy stuffing

Size:

18.5cm (7¼in) circumference

Instructions:

Using yarn A, cast on 13 sts.

Row 1 (WS): p to end.

Row 2: (kfb) to end (26 sts).

Row 3: p to end.

Row 4: (kfb) to last st, k1 (51 sts).

Rows 5 and 6: beg with a p WS row, work 2 rows in st st. Break yarn A.

Rows 7–24: work rows 1–18 of chart.

Note: the first row of the chart is a WS row; WS rows are read from left to right and RS rows from right to left.

Break yarns B and C.

Row 25: using yarn A, p to end.

Row 26: (k2tog) to last st, k1 (26 sts).

Row 27: p to end.

Row 28: (k2tog) to end (13 sts).

Row 29: p to end.

Row 30: (k2tog) to last st, k1 (7 sts).

Break yarn, thread through all sts and pull tightly.

Fasten off.

To make up

Sew the side seam and stuff. Attach some yellow yarn or cord to the top of the bauble and tie the ends at the desired length.

Chart

■ Yarn B □ Yarn C

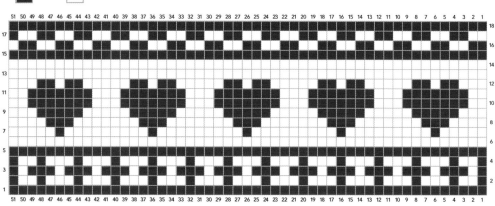

Penguin

Materials:

6m (6½yd) each of DK (8-ply/light worsted) yarn in black (A) and white (B), and small amounts in yellow (C), light blue (D) and blue (E)

Small amount of DK (8-ply/light worsted) yarn or 4-ply (fingering) yarn in lilac felted tweed (F)

Small length of strong white cotton thread

Small amount of toy stuffing

Size:

7cm (2¾in) tall

Instructions:

Body

Using yarn A, cast on 10 sts.

Row 1 (WS): p to end.

Row 2: (kfb) to end (20 sts).

Row 3: p to end.

Row 4: (k1, kfb) to end (30 sts).

Row 5: p to end.

Row 6: using yarn A k9, using yarn B k12, using yarn A k9.

Row 7–19: changing colours as set and beg with a p WS row, work 13 rows in st st.

Row 20: keeping colours correct, (k1, k2tog) to end (20 sts). Break yarn B.

Rows 21–29: using yarn A and beg with a p WS row, work 9 rows in st st.

Row 30: (k2tog) to end (10 sts).

Break yarn, thread through all sts and pull tightly.

Fasten off.

Wings: make two

Using yarn A, cast on 12 sts.

Rows 1–3: beg with a p WS row, work 3 rows in st st.

Row 4: (k2, k2tog) to end (9 sts).

Row 5: p to end.

Row 6: (k1, k2tog) to end (6 sts).

Row 7: (p2tog) to end (3 sts).

Break yarn, thread through all sts and pull tightly. Fasten off.

Beak

Using yarn C, cast on 5 sts.

Row 1: p to end.

Row 2: skpo, k1, k2tog (3 sts).

Row 3: p3tog (1 st).

Fasten off.

Hat

Using yarn D, cast on 20 sts.

Rows 1–4: beg with a p WS row, work 4 rows in st st.

Rows 5 and 6: change to yarn E and, beg with a p WS row, work 2 rows in st st.

Row 7: change to yarn D, p to end.

Row 8: using yarn D, (k2, k2tog) to end (15 sts).

Row 9: change to yarn E, p to end.

Row 10: using yarn E, (k1, k2tog) to end (10 sts).

Break yarn, thread through all sts and pull tightly.

Fasten off.

Scarf

Using yarn F, cast on 3 sts. Work in g st until the piece measures 15cm (6in).

Cast off.

Pompom

Wind yarn B 20 times around two fingers and tie the centre with strong cotton thread. Cut the loops open and trim to shape.

To make up

With the fastened-off yarn end of the body, sew the seam half closed. With the cast-on yarn end, work a running stitch along the cast-on edge and pull tightly to gather. Sew the rest of the base seam, stuff the body and close the seam. Seam the wings and attach them to the sides of the body. Attach the cast-on edge of the beak to the face. Seam the hat, lightly stuff and attach it to the head. Sew the pompom onto the hat. Using yarn B, work a French knot for each eye. Make backstitches along the short ends of the scarf, leaving a loop every other stitch. Cut the loops open and trim. Sew the scarf around the neck.

Robin

Materials:

10m (11yd) of DK (8-ply/light worsted) yarn in brown (A) and small amounts in red (B), sea green (C), green (D) and dark brown (E)

Small amount of toy stuffing

Additional equipment:

2.75mm (UK 12, US 2) DPN to make i-cord

Size:

8cm (3in)

Instructions:

Body

Using yarn A, cast on 10 sts.

Row 1 (WS): p to end.

Row 2: (kfb) to end (20 sts).

Row 3: p to end.

Row 4: (k1, kfb) to end (30 sts).

Rows 5–17: beg with a p WS row, work 13 rows in st st.

Row 18: (k1, k2tog) to end (20 sts).

Row 19: p to end.

Row 20: (k2tog) to end (10 sts).

Break yarn, thread through all sts and pull tightly. Fasten off.

Tummy

Using yarn B, cast on 10 sts.

Works rows 1–4 as given for body (30 sts).

Row 5: p to end.

Cast off.

Wings: make two

Using yarn A, cast on 8 sts.

Rows 1–3: beg with a p WS row, work 3 rows in st st.

Row 4: (k2, k2tog) to end (6 sts).

Row 5: p to end.

Row 6: (k2tog) to end (3 sts).

Break yarn, thread through all sts and pull tightly. Fasten off.

Hat

Using yarn C, cast on 26 sts.

Row 1 (RS): k to end.

Rows 2 and 3: change to yarn D and, beg with a p WS row, work 2 rows in st st.

Row 4: change to yarn C, p to end.

Row 5: using yarn C, k2, (k2tog, k2) to end (20 sts).

Rows 6 and 7: change to yarn D and, beg with a p WS row, work 2 rows in st st. Break yarn D.

Row 8: using yarn C, p to end.

Row 9: k2tog, (k1, k2tog) to end (13 sts).

Rows 10–13: beg with a p WS row, work 4 rows in st st.

Row 14: (p2tog) to last st, p1 (7 sts).

Break yarn, thread through all sts and pull tightly. Fasten off.

Beak

Using yarn E, cast on 6 sts.

Row 1: p to end.

Row 2: (k2tog) to end (3 sts).

Break yarn, thread through all sts and pull tightly. Fasten off.

Legs: make two

Using yarn E, cast on 3 sts. Work an i-cord for 5 rows.

Cast on 2 sts, cast off 3 sts (the 2 cast-on sts and 1 original st) (2 sts).

Cast on 2 sts, cast off 3 sts (the 2 cast-on sts and 1 original st) (1 st).

Cast on 2 sts, cast off all sts.

To make up

Sew the body seam and stuff. Seam the wings and attach
them to the sides of the body. Sew the side seam of the
tummy and attach it to the front of the body. Seam the beak
from the fastened-off yarn end and sew the cast-on edge
to the face. Using yarn E, work a French knot for each eye.
Attach the legs to the bottom of the body. Seam the hat,
lightly stuff and attach it to the head. Attach a loop of
yarn C to the top of the hat for hanging.

Finger Puppets

Materials:

For Santa: 8m (9yd) of DK (8-ply/light worsted) yarn in red (B) and small amounts in white (A), pale pink (C) and dark brown (E)

Small amount of chunky (bulky) fleecy yarn in white (D)

Small amount of toy stuffing

For Rudolf: 10m (11yd) of DK (8-ply/light worsted) yarn in brown (F) and small amounts in red (B) and dark brown (E)

1cm (½in) diameter gold bell

Small amount of toy stuffing

Additional equipment:

2.75mm (UK 12, US 2) DPN to make i-cord

Size:

Santa: 9cm (3½in) long

Rudolf: 11cm (4½in) long

Instructions:

Santa's body and head

Using yarn A, cast on 23 sts.

Row 1 (RS): (k1, p1) to last st, k1.

Row 2: (p1, k1) to last st, p1.

Rows 3 and 4: rep rows 1 and 2 once more. Break yarn A.

Rows 5–22: change to yarn B and, beg with a k RS row, work 18 rows in st st.

Row 23 (shape neck): k2tog, (k1, k2tog) to end (15 sts). Break yarn B.

Row 24: change to yarn C and p to end.

Row 25: k5, (kfb) five times, k5 (20 sts).

Rows 26–29: beg with a p WS row, work 4 rows in st st.

Row 30 (shape eyeline): p4, (p2tog, p1) four times, p4 (16 sts).

Rows 31–33: beg with a k RS row, work 3 rows in st st.

Row 34: (p2, p2tog) to end (12 sts).

Break yarn, thread through all sts and pull tightly. Fasten off.

Hat

Using yarn A, cast on 20 sts.

Rows 1–4: beg with a k RS row, work 4 rows in st st. Break yarn A.

Rows 5–8: change to yarn B and, beg with a k RS row, work 4 rows in st st.

Row 9: (k2, k2tog) to end (15 sts).

Rows 10–14: beg with a p WS row, work 5 rows in st st.

Row 15: (k1, k2tog) to end (10 sts).

Row 16: p to end.

Row 17: (k2tog) to end (5 sts).

Break yarn, thread through all sts and pull tightly. Fasten off.

Beard

Using yarn D, cast on 10 sts.

Row 1: k to end.

Row 2: skpo, k to last 2 sts, k2tog (8 sts).

Rows 3–5: rep row 2 three more times (2 sts).

Row 6: k2tog (1 st).

Fasten off.

To make up

With the fastened-off yarn end, sew the body seam closed from the head down to the neck. Keep this yarn end free at the neck. Sew the body seam closed from the base and stuff the head. With the yarn C tail end left at the neck, work a running stitch around the neck and pull tightly to gather. With the same yarn, work a running stitch over the eyeline and pull gently to shape a dent. Using yarn C, make a French knot for the nose. Seam the hat and attach it to the head. Sew the beard in place on the face. Using yarn E, work a French knot for each eye. With yarn D, make backstitches under the nose for the moustache.

Rudolf's body and head

Using yarn F, cast on 23 sts. Work rows 1–29 as given for Santa finger puppet, using yarn F only throughout.

Rows 30–32: beg with a p WS row, work 3 rows in st st.

Row 33 (shape eyeline): k4, (k2tog, k1) four times, k4 (16 sts).

Rows 34–37: beg with a p WS row, work 4 rows in st st.

Row 38: (p2, p2tog) to end (12 sts).

Break yarn, thread through all sts and pull tightly. Fasten off.

Nose

Using yarn B, cast on 10 sts. Break yarn, thread through all sts and pull tightly. Fasten off.

Stitch the sides together to create a nose.

Ears: make two

Using yarn F, cast on 4 sts.

Row 1: p to end.

Row 2: (k2tog) twice (2 sts).

Row 3: p2tog (1 st).

Fasten off.

Long antlers: make two

Using yarn E, cast on 3 sts. Work an i-cord for 7 rows. Break yarn, thread through all sts and pull tightly. Fasten off.

Short antlers: make two

Using yarn E, cast on 3 sts. Work an i-cord for 4 rows. Break yarn, thread through all sts and pull tightly. Fasten off. Sew one short piece to the side of each long piece.

To make up

Make up the body and head as given for the Santa finger puppet. Sew the nose and antlers onto the head. Using yarn C, work a French knot for each eye. Thread the bell through a strand of yarn B and tie it around the neck.

Snowman

Materials:

12m (13yd) of DK (8-ply/light worsted) yarn in white (A) and small amounts in red brown (B), orange (C), dark brown (D) and blue felted tweed (E)

Small amount of toy stuffing

Size:

10cm (4in)

Instructions:

Body

Using yarn A, cast on 10 sts.

Row 1 (WS): p to end.

Row 2: (kfb) to end (20 sts).

Row 3: p to end.

Row 4: (k1, kfb) to end (30 sts).

Row 5: p to end.

Row 6: (k2, kfb) to end (40 sts).

Row 7: p to end.

Row 8 (g st ridge): p to end.

Rows 9–27: beg with a p WS row, work 19 rows in st st.

Row 28 (shape neck): (k2tog) to end (20 sts).

Row 29: p to end.

Row 30: (k2, kfb) six times, k2 (26 sts).

Rows 31–40: beg with a p WS row, work 10 rows in st st.

Row 41: (k2tog) to end (13 sts).

Break yarn, thread through all sts and pull tightly.

Fasten off.

Arms: make two

Using yarn A, cast on 7 sts. Beg with a p WS row, work 8 rows in st st.

Break yarn, thread through all sts and pull tightly. Fasten off.

Hat

Using yarn B, cast on 10 sts.

Row 1 (WS): p to end.

Row 2: (kfb) to end (20 sts).

Rows 3–6: beg with a p WS row, work 4 rows in st st.

Row 7 (g st ridge): k to end.

Row 8: (kfb) to end (40 sts).

Cast off.

Nose

Using yarn C, cast on 5 sts.

Row 1 (WS): p to end.

Row 2: skpo, k1, k2tog (3 sts).

Row 3: p1, p2tog (2 sts).

Row 4: k2tog (1 st).

Fasten off.

Buttons: make two

Using yarn D, cast on 4 sts. Break yarn, thread through all sts and pull tightly. Fasten off.

Stitch the sides together to create a bobble.

Scarf

Using yarn E, cast on 4 sts leaving a long end. Work in garter stitch until the piece measures 15cm (6in). Cast off, leaving a long end. Thread a needle with the yarn end and backstitch along the short edge a few times, leaving a loop every other stitch. Cut the loops open to make the fringe. Repeat for the other edge.

To make up

With the fastened-off yarn end, sew the body seam closed from the head down to the neck. Keep this yarn end free at the neck. With the cast-on yarn end, work a running stitch along the cast-on edge of the body and pull tightly to gather. Sew the body closed from the base up to the waist. Stuff and sew the rest of the body seam closed, avoiding the neck area. With the yarn A end left at the neck, work a running stitch around the neck and pull tightly to gather. Thread a needle with yarn A and insert it from the centre of the base, taking the needle out at the back of the body. Repeat with the other yarn end and pull on the yarn ends to flatten the base. Seam the arms, nose and hat and sew them in place on the body. Attach the buttons to the front of the body. Using yarn D, work a French knot for each eye and embroider the mouth with short backstitches. Attach the scarf around the neck.

Christmas Fairy

Materials:

10m (11yd) of DK (8-ply/light worsted) yarn in red (A),
   6m (6½yd) in pale pink (B) and green (C), small
   amounts in yellow (D) and dark brown (E)

Small amount of white fleecy yarn (F)

Small amount of toy stuffing

Additional equipment:

2.75mm (UK 12, US 2) DPN to make i-cord

Size:

12cm (4¾in) tall

Instructions:

Body and head

Using yarn A, cast on 9 sts.

Row 1 (WS): p to end.

Row 2: (kfb) to end (18 sts).

Rows 3–15: beg with a p WS row, work 13 rows in st st.

Row 16 (shape neck): (k1, k2tog) to end (12 sts).

Row 17: change to yarn B and p to end.

Row 18: k3, (kfb) six times, k3 (18 sts).

Rows 19–22: beg with a p WS row, work 4 rows in st st.

Row 23 (shape eyeline): p3, (p2tog, p1) four times, p3 (14 sts).

Rows 24–26: beg with a k RS row, work 3 rows in st st.

Row 27: k2, (k2tog, k2) to end (11 sts).

Break yarn, thread through all sts and pull tightly.

Fasten off.

Petals for skirt: make six

Make three each in yarns A and C.

Cast on 8 sts.

Rows 1–7: beg with a p WS row, work 7 rows in st st.

Row 8: skpo, k to last 2 sts, k2tog (6 sts).

Row 9: p to end.

Rows 10 and 11: rep rows 8 and 9 once more (4 sts).

Row 12: skpo, k2tog (2 sts).

Row 13: p2tog (1 st).

Fasten off.

Sleeves: make two

Using yarn C, cast on 8 sts. Beg with a p WS row, work 2 rows in st st.

Break yarn, thread through all sts and pull tightly.

Fasten off.

Arms: make two

Using yarn B, cast on 3 sts. Work an i-cord for 6 rows.

Break yarn, thread through all sts and pull tightly.

Fasten off.

Legs: make two

Work as given for the elf (see page 22), using yarn A for the shoe and yarn B for the leg.

Hat

Work as given for the elf (see page 22), using yarn C (for the brim) and yarn A.

To make up

With the fastened-off yarn end, sew the body seam closed from the head down to the neck. Keep this yarn end free at the neck. With the cast-on yarn end, work a running stitch along the cast-on edge of the body and pull tightly to gather. Sew the body closed from the base up to the waist. Stuff and sew the rest of the body seam closed, avoiding the neck area. With the yarn B tail end left at the neck, work a running stitch around the neck and pull tightly to gather. With the same yarn, work a running stitch on the face over the eyeline and pull gently to shape a dent. Using yarn B, make a French knot for the nose. Seam the legs and attach them to the base of the body. Attach the skirt petal pieces to the waist. Wrap each sleeve around one end of each arm and secure the sleeves in place, then sew the seam and attach each arm to the body. Seam the hat and sew it onto the head. For the hair, thread a needle with yarn D and pierce the head from one side to the other, leaving long loops. Wrap the hair with yarn A and secure the wrap with a few stitches, then cut the loops. Make smaller loops with backstitches for the fringe. Using yarn E, work a French knot for each eye. Wrap a length of yarn F around the neck and stitch in place.

Toy Soldiers

Materials:

For one soldier: 6m (6½yd) of DK (8-ply/light worsted) yarn in white (B), 4m (4½yd) in dark brown (A), light beige (C) and red or green (for the jacket) (D); and a small amount in golden yellow (E)

Small amount of toy stuffing

Additional equipment:

3mm (UK 3, US 11) crochet hook
2.75mm (UK 12, US 2) DPN to make i-cord

Size:

10cm (4in)

Instructions:

Feet, legs, body and head

This is knitted in one piece.

Using yarn A, cast on 8 sts.

Row 1 (WS): p to end.

Row 2: (kfb) to end (16 sts).

Row 3: p to end.

Row 4 (g st ridge): p to end. Break yarn A.

Rows 5–25: change to yarn B and, beg with a p WS row, work 21 rows in st st.

Row 26 (shape neck): k1, (k2tog, k1) to end (11 sts).

Row 27: change to yarn C and p to end.

Row 28: k2, (kfb) seven times, k2 (18 sts).

Rows 29–31: beg with a p WS row, work 3 rows in st st.

Row 32 (shape eyeline): k3, (k2tog, k1) four times, k3 (14 sts).

Rows 33–35: beg with a p WS row, work 3 rows in st st.

Row 36: k2, (k2tog, k2) to end (11 sts).

Break yarn, thread through all sts and pull tightly. Fasten off.

Jacket

Using yarn D, cast on 20 sts. Beg with a p WS row, work 12 rows in st st.

Next row: (p2tog) to end (10 sts).

Break yarn, thread through all sts and pull tightly. Fasten off.

Shoulder pads: make two

Using yarn E, cast on 10 sts. Beg with a p WS row, work 2 rows in st st.

Break yarn, thread through all sts and pull tightly. Fasten off.

Arms: make two

Using yarn D, cast on 4 sts. Work an i-cord for 5 rows. Change to yarn C and work an i-cord for 2 more rows. Break yarn, thread through all sts and pull tightly. Fasten off.

Hat

Using yarn A, cast on 9 sts.

Row 1 (WS): p to end.

Row 2: (kfb) to end (18 sts).

Row 3: p to end.

Row 4 (g st ridge): p to end.

Rows 5–11: beg with a p WS row, work 7 rows in st st.

Cast off.

Belt

Using yarn A and a crochet hook, make 16 chains.

Fasten off.

Sashes: make two

This is for the green soldier only.

Using yarn B and a crochet hook, make 12 chains.

Fasten off.

To make up

With the cast-on yarn end of the body, work a running stitch along the cast-on edge and pull tightly to gather. Sew the base and body seam half closed. With the fastened-off yarn end, sew the head seam and stuff the body, avoiding the neck area. Using yarn C, work a running stitch around the neck and pull tightly to gather. With the same yarn, work a running stitch over the eyeline and pull gently to shape a dent. Using yarn C, make a French knot for the nose. Wrap the jacket around the body, and sew it closed, with the seam at the back. Thread a needle with a length of yarn B and pierce through the centre of the lower body, working a vertical line of tight stitches to create the impression of legs. Seam the shoulder pads and sew one in place over each arm. Attach the arms to the side of the body. Secure the belt around the waist. For the red soldier, using yarn B, make two French knots for buttons on the chest. For the green soldier, attach the sashes, crossing them over the chest. Using yarn A, work a French knot for each eye. Seam the hat, stuff, and attach it to the head. Create the hat strap with a length of yarn A. Attach a loop of yarn E to the top of the hat for hanging.

Angel

Materials:

For one angel: 8m (9yd) each of DK (8-ply/light worsted) yarn in red (A), sky blue (B) and white (D) and small amounts in pale pink (C), honey yellow (F) and dark brown (G)

6m (6½yd) of chunky (bulky) fleecy yarn in white (E)

Small amount of 4-ply (fingering) yarn in red (H)

Small amount of toy stuffing

Instructions:

Note: yarns A, B and D can be swapped around to create various colour combinations.

Body and head

Using yarn A, cast on 8 sts.

Row 1 (WS): p to end.

Row 2: (kfb) to end (16 sts).

Row 3: p to end.

Row 4: (k1, kfb) to end (24 sts).

Row 5: p to end.

Row 6 (g st ridge): p to end.

Row 7: p to end.

Rows 8 and 9: change to yarn B, beg with a k RS row, work 2 rows in st st.

Row 10: (using yarn B k3, using yarn A k1) to end.

Row 11: using yarn B p2, (using yarn B p1, using yarn A p1) to last 2 sts, using yarn B p2.

Row 12: rep row 10. Break yarn A.

Rows 13–15: using yarn B, beg with a p WS row, work 3 rows in st st.

Row 16: (k2, k2tog) to end (18 sts).

Rows 17–21: beg with a p WS row, work 5 rows in st st.

Row 22 (shape neck): (k1, k2tog) to end (12 sts). Break yarn B.

Row 23: change to yarn C and p to end.

Row 24: k3, (kfb) six times, k3 (18 sts).

Rows 25–27: beg with a p WS row, work 3 rows in st st.

Row 28 (shape eyeline): k3, (k2tog, k1) four times, k3 (14 sts).

Rows 29–31: beg with a p WS row, work 3 rows in st st.

Row 32: k2, (k2tog, k2) to end (11 sts).

Break yarn, thread through all sts and pull tightly.

Fasten off.

Additional equipment:

4mm (UK 8, US 6) knitting needles

Size:

7cm (2¾in) tall

Cape

Using yarn D, cast on 24 sts.

Rows 1–3: k to end.

Row 4 (WS): k2, p to last 2 sts, k2.

Row 5: k to end.

Row 6: rep row 4.

Row 7: (k1, k2tog) to end (16 sts).

Rows 8–10: beg with a p WS row, work 3 rows in st st.

Row 11: (k2, k2tog) to end (12 sts).

Cast off.

Hat

Using yarn A, cast on 18 sts.

Rows 1–9: beg with a p WS row, work 9 rows in st st.

Row 10: k2, (k2tog, k2) to end (14 sts).

Rows 11–13: beg with a p WS row, work 3 rows in st st.

Row 14: (k2tog) to end (7 sts).

Break yarn, thread through all sts and pull tightly.

Fasten off.

Wings: make two

Using yarn E and 4mm (UK 8, US 6) needles, cast on 8 sts.

Rows 1 and 2: k to end.

Row 3: skpo, k to end (7 sts).

Row 4: k to end.

Row 5: skpo, k to end (6 sts).

Row 6: k to end.

Row 7: skpo, k to end (5 sts).

Cast off.

To make up

With the fastened-off yarn end, sew the body seam closed from the head down to the neck. Keep this yarn end free at the neck. With the cast-on yarn end, work a running stitch along the cast-on edge of the body and pull tightly to gather. Sew the body closed from the base up to the waist. Stuff and sew the rest of the body seam closed. With the yarn C tail end of yarn left at the neck, work a running stitch around the neck and pull tightly to gather. With the same yarn, work a running stitch on the face over the eyeline and pull gently to shape a dent. Using yarn C, make a French knot for the nose. Thread a needle with yarn A and insert it from the centre of the base, taking the needle out at the

back of the body. Repeat with the other yarn end and pull on the yarn ends to flatten the base. Wrap the cape around the body and secure at the neck.

To make the hair, thread a needle with two strands taken from yarn F and work backstitches on the head, leaving a loop every other stitch – leave short loops at the forehead and long loops at the sides. Cut the long side loops open and trim the ends if desired. Seam and attach the hat to the head. Attach the wings to the back of the body. Using yarn G, work a French knot for each eye. Thread a needle with a length of yarn H and make a bow at the chin, securing with a few stitches.

Cat in a Basket

Materials:

12m (13yd) of DK (8-ply/light worsted) yarn in grey (A) and 16m (17½yd) in mink (B)

Small amounts of 4-ply (fingering) yarn in dark brown (C) and pink (D)

Small amount of toy stuffing

Size:

7cm (2¾in) long

Instructions:

Body and front legs

Using yarn A, cast on 8 sts.

Row 1 (WS): p to end.

Row 2: (kfb) to end (16 sts).

Row 3: p to end.

Row 4: (kfb) to end (32 sts).

Rows 5–11: beg with a p WS row, work 7 rows in st st.

Row 12: (k2, k2tog) to end (24 sts).

Rep rows 5–12 once more (18 sts).

Next row: p to end.

Cast off.

Head

Using yarn A, cast on 10 sts.

Row 1 (WS): p to end.

Row 2: (kfb) to end (20 sts).

Rows 3–7: beg with a p WS row, work 5 rows in st st.

Row 8: k6, (k2tog) four times, k6 (16 sts).

Rows 9–12: beg with a p WS row, work 4 rows in st st.

Row 13: (p2tog) to end (8 sts).

Break yarn, thread through all sts and pull tightly.

Fasten off.

Ears: make two

Using yarn A, cast on 3 sts.

Row 1: p2tog, p1 (2 sts).

Row 2: skpo (1 st).

Fasten off.

Tail

Using yarn A, cast on 8 sts. Beg with a p WS row, work 15 rows in st st.

Break yarn, thread through all sts and pull tightly.

Fasten off.

To make up

With the cast-on yarn end of the body, work a running stitch along the cast-on edge and pull tightly to gather. Sew the body half closed with the same yarn end. Fold one cast-off edge corner inwards and sew to 2cm (¾in) from the tip to create the front leg. Repeat for the other leg. Sew the tummy and stuff, then close the seam. Stitch the tips of the front legs together. Seam the head, stuff and sew the head onto the body. Sew the cast-on edge of the ears onto the head. Seam the tail and attach it to the body. Using yarn C, embroider the eyes and nose with backstitches. Using yarn D, backstitch three whiskers on either side.

Basket

Using yarn B, cast on 20 sts.

Row 1 (WS): p to end.

Row 2: (k1, kfb) to end (30 sts).

Row 3: p to end.

Row 4: (k2, kfb) to end (40 sts).

Row 5: p to end.

Row 6: (k3, kfb) to end (50 sts).

Row 7: p to end.

Row 8: (k4, kfb) to end (60 sts).

Row 9: p to end.

Row 10 (g st ridge): p to end.

Rows 11–18: beg with a p WS row, work 8 rows in st st.

Row 19 (g st ridge): k to end.

Row 20: (k4, k2tog) to end (50 sts).

Rows 21–26: beg with a p WS row, work 6 rows in st st.

Cast off purlwise.

To make up

With the cast-on yarn end, work a running stitch along the cast-on edge and pull tightly to gather. Sew the base and side seam. Fold at the garter stitch ridge fold line and sew the cast-off edge to the inner base edge.

Christmas Pudding

Materials:

12m (13yd) of DK (8-ply/light worsted) yarn in dark brown (A) and small amounts in green (C) and red (D)

Small amount of chunky (bulky) fleecy yarn in white (B)

Small amount of toy stuffing

Additional equipment:

3.5mm (UK 9/10, US 4) knitting needles for the cream

Size:

18cm (7in) circumference

Instructions:

Note: All parts are knitted with 2.75mm (UK 12, US 2) needles except the cream.

Pudding

Using yarn A, cast on 9 sts.

Row 1 (WS): p to end.

Row 2: (kfb) to end (18 sts).

Row 3: p to end.

Row 4: (k1, kfb) to end (27 sts).

Row 5: p to end.

Row 6: (k2, kfb) to end (36 sts).

Row 7: p to end.

Row 8: (k3, kfb) to end (45 sts).

Rows 9–21: beg with a p WS row, work 13 rows in st st.

Row 22: (k3, k2tog) to end (36 sts).

Row 23: p to end.

Row 24: (k2, k2tog) to end (27 sts).

Row 25: p to end.

Row 26: (k1, k2tog) to end (18 sts).

Row 27: p to end.

Row 28: (k2tog) to end (9 sts).

Break yarn, thread through all sts and pull tightly.
Fasten off.

Cream

Using yarn B and 3.5mm (UK 9/10, US 4) needles, cast on 27 sts.

Rows 1–3: k to end.

Row 4: (k1, k2tog) to end (18 sts).

Rows 5 and 6: k to end.

Row 7: (k2tog) to end (9 sts).

Break yarn, thread through all sts and pull tightly.
Fasten off.

Leaves: make two

Using yarn C, cast on 7 sts.

Rows 1–4: k to end.

Row 5: k2tog, k to last 2 sts, k2tog (5 sts).

Row 6: k to end.

Rows 7 and 8: rep rows 5 and 6 (3 sts).

Row 9: k2tog, k1 (2 sts).

Pass first st over the second and fasten off.

Berries: make two

Using yarn D, cast on 10 sts. Beg with a p WS row, work 2 rows in st st.

Break yarn, thread through all sts and pull tightly. Fasten off.
Stitch the sides together to create a berry.

To make up

Seam the pudding and stuff. Sew the side edges of the cream and attach to the pudding. Sew the leaves and berries in place on top of the cream.

Acknowledgements

I would like to thank everyone on the Search Press team, especially Katie French and May Corfield, for helping me to create such a wonderful book. I would also like to thank the designers, Juan Hayward and Emma Sutcliffe, for the beautiful layout and the photographer, Fiona Murray, for the lovely photography. Thanks also go to Jemima Bicknell for her pattern checking.